HALF LIGHT

By

Ari Augustine

ANEMOIA

Visit author's website at: www.ariaugustine.com
Visit Dragons at www.teacupdragon.org

Published by: Ari Augustine & Anemoia Press & Teacup Dragons
Identifiers: ISBN 979-8-218-07093-9 (paperback) | ASIN B0BDPVCHN5 (digital)

Subjects: Poetry

Book cover design:
Ari Augustine | www.ariaugustine.com
Book interior design:
K. J. Harrowick | www.authorkjharrowick.com

TABLE OF CONTENTS

HALF LIGHT

LETTER OF CAUTION

Dear reader,

I had no intention of writing these poems; they were a momentary catharsis that I had planned to burn and bury the second they brought release. I began jotting them down in between sessions with a trauma specialist, and there was no expectation that they would see the light of day. But ghosts have no concept of time or place, and when unsettled, they do not quiet easily.

If you've read *Elsewhere, We Became,* you might expect this collection to be silver-lined. You might hope it is filled with a fondness for life, shifting views of love, and odes to self-discovery. But please heed my warning: this is far from the case in *Half Light.*

Half Light is written from a place of grief; it heavily features nuanced references to the following: physical and psychological abuse, addiction, death, homicidal/suicidal ideation, mental illness, and dysfunctional families. These are often written with complex and nuanced language that might not make sense to most readers, but may be triggering for those with PTSD related to persistent childhood trauma.

Though this may not make sense to you, there's a comfort in meeting with negative memories. There is solace in holding them in your arms; there is clarity in seeing them for all their sufferings and joys; there is peace in giving them kindness and understanding. But the process of consciousness begins with pain.

We must be willing to rip open old wounds to examine them; we must divine the truth out of riddles, fragmented memories, and lies we've swallowed whole; we must be willing to embrace the fact that we didn't survive the depths of darkness unscathed. That we are not good or bad. That whatever the sum of us, whatever we've become in the shadows, it's okay.

Half Light is not for everyone, but I thank you anyways for picking up this sliver of my heart and having the courage to journey into its pages.

Always,

Ari Augustine

DEDICATION

For Leslie and all the other girls

raised by wolves.

Part I.
CLAY

CHILDREN OF
ARES

War was our mother tongue.

Rooted in gunpowder silt,

We grew from the ruins.

It was milk of inherited fury,

Ordinary words imprisoned to pages,

wound in red,

Air to lungs & water to lips.

It was the needle & the thread,

& through creation, undoing.

They say it's all we know.

PROMETHEUS

It was a dream we forged together,

pitiful hearts huddled around the dying

ember of the pit that spat us out.

We would breathe fire

We would temper flesh

We would sharpen tongues

We would greedily break

again, again, again

If only to become more

than the clay you abandoned

A PLAYLIST
OF
FONDNESS
AND
AFFECTION

1. Sipping Sulfur Water Like Holy Wine
2. Sitting In the Darkness of Our Skins
3. Staring Into Mud Pies to Make Sense of the Divine
4. Inhaling Embers & Smoke In a Ritual
5. As if it'll breathe life into us
6. We were all there in Cook's Forest
7. Desperate children
8. Feeding trespassing wolves within
9. Blood in the river, bones in the wind
10. Shivering, feverish, starved
11. For Damnation, Salvation
12. Singing sweet sorrows to the dirt
13. Our labors are not in vain
14. Names carved into tree trunks
15. Clothing strung over branches
16. Memories in moonlight
17. Confessions, gone by dawn
18. Holy wine, sweet & soured mouths
19. Full to the brim, darling
20. Of loneliness and loss

21. There was love, we think
22. When the darkness swallowed us whole

APPALACHIA

We inherited the black mountain and its woes
from our grandfather / it is sprawled beneath the
sulfur sky like a drunkard / naked of all pretense
/ silent and lonely / singing to the wind / clinging
to the forest / begging the earth beneath our feet
to hold it / none-too-gently / we cannot forget /
that eerie morning / the gray fog blanketing its
north face / purple rain spitting in the east / fires
raging in the south / everything west was barren /
the only hope was up or down / but we are
tethered to this place / we clawed our way to its
peak / desperate / tired / hungry, hungry, hungry
/ burrowed our hearts in a cave / black lungs /
cloudy vision /bloody teeth / scuffed hands /
numb and hardened / there is no where else to go
/ we inherited this mountain / and we will tend to
its woes.

PAPERCUTS

There's a place in our bones where
We've buried you, a shallow grave
between yesterday and today
        that will never overgrow with
flowers.
There's silence trapped behind our teeth
because wounding you with sharp words
would mean wounding us.
        And we're so weary from
breaking.
We feel every fissure,
every crack you pried open,
like a rusty door that won't fully shut.
No matter how carefully you tread,
        the staircase moans a warning.
Remember. Remember. Remember.
Do you know how badly
We've wished that only goodness
        was born from these ruins?

Grief is a fountain that never runs clean...

A HUM OF WELCOMED FALSEHOODS, EXAMINED

"We" is a congregation of chipped chairs stacked haphazardly on a lacquered table

Essentially a disrupted series of womanhood: child, mamaw, daughter, mother

"We" as a dance of the subtext of a language varying in fluidity and fluency

Essentially an interrogation of lies and betrayal sewn behind the flesh of family

"We" as fatal flaws seeped deep into dry walls, where we drew our dreams

Essentially a coded message to the past: the love map is inaccurate, abort mission

"We" as a prayer uttered with parted, painted lips, together always out of love

Essentially a garden ripe with fruit that will never sate our hunger or quell despair

"We" as a performance of function and ego: rules, roles, recreation, redemption

Essentially the bending of light across unsteady waters, blinding our gaze to horror

"We" as a sacred refuge of familiarity & comfort & blood & white lies & forgiveness

Essentially the unraveling of self at a knotted junction, we are what we secretly hate

"We" as a prequel to escapism & devotion to nihilism & a departure from childhood

Essentially the act of dying again and again to avoid our ill-fated ties to this world

"We" as a violation of nature & premonition of sacrifice & the undoing of the past

Essentially a congregation of lies we devour to survive the plight of family

Forgiveness is loving ourselves enough
to stop letting our expectations of the
past control the present.

Part II.
RUST

This is how you
made us.

This is how you

ˑsn ʇɟǝl

This is how we

learned to live.

We were lonely creatures

crawling from the iron grave

hands hungrier than our mouths

for a bit of flesh to call ours

 The word for mother was "Why"

but our pitiful tongues couldn't

taste it shape it own it

so we grew into wolves,

howling at moons we couldn't touch.

you wanted the me who didn't know

you weren't the center of the universe.

i wanted to believe you were.

LETTER XII

You wound us

again

again

again

as if we were a home built

to be battered

and torn apart

by the path

of a tornado.

TOO PATIENT,
TOO BRIGHT

We waited for you the way waves
reach for the shore

the way autumn air rustles through
leaves at night

the way dawn stretches over fields,
burning, longing

the way rain seeps into earth,
breathing, drowning

the way storms rumble the distance,
unsettled, eager

We waited for you, always,
but you never came.

BLIND FAITH

We have paid:	the blood on our knees
For the sins of:	wet the floors between pews
Our fathers:	our hands clasp in a begging
The night:	"O, Sacred Divine…"
Consumes:	but we are already lost

A CATALOG OF BODIES

there is a chemical taste we cannot wash out of our teeth / the rose bush is a dried husk of thorns in the morning / the pine needles sing beneath the spark of a lighter / the funeral procession dances to the roar of a mower / the divines smell of kerosene, burnt wood, and grease / water tastes of blood copper and rotten pickled eggs / the bodies gleam amid their tight-rope dances

twisted limbs as crooked as roots buried in the
earth / eyes sunken deep as cavernous limestone
sinkholes / bones popping like rogue bullets in an
empty house / the carpet is soaked with alcohol
the air is curdled milk, cold coffee, the dregs of
smoke / the bodies are poised in awkward angles
working, playing, comforting, hurting, transfixed
the teeth glint in the sunlight like pearls / mouths
bared wide as if in a smile, a gnashing grimace
who can say why these creatures remain / in the
vicious decay of the halls they once built

SPLINTERED

We believe in: lies, betrayal, altered memories

the smallest acts: motherhood, undone

of kindness: slowing murdering our hopes

to make sense: promises, promises, promises

of cruelty: Is this that all you gave us?

Slowly, surely, silently, we become

our own thoughts.

Part III.
BLOOD

To us

you were the shining

moon our hands

were too small

to hold

PARADISE

We know the emptiness of
the well
the stones of regret that
have built it
the hands that have bled,
bruised, blistered
the voice raw from shouting
down its cobbled throat
the fluttering lungs which
have flailed, desperate
the eyes swollen and
swallowed by darkness

LOST

the soil so rusted red it almost

looks like blood

the letters we folded into the

cracks, our memories

gone with the faded ink, at last

"alive, alive, alive" is the only

answer to our questions

the only proof we are still

hunting for

that heaven we were promised.

A LIST OF
DEVOTION
AND DESPAIR

the sum of our relationship is disappointment /
the average of our love is devotion and despair /
there is no beginning or end to the umbilical cord
/ it is a noose of delight and desperation / you
shaped us out of clay / your desires reflected / our
eyes of wind and fire / lungs of dreams / hearts of
lightning / laughter of summer rain / wishes
manifest from the kiln / your hands were warm /
once / tender / tempered / softly hesitant / our
mother, divine / we had no need of anything else
/ all gods are prone to jealousy / a fatal flaw / fire
is quick to burn / wind is fleeting / water drowns
/ dreams die / lightening, despite odds, always
finds a way to strike twice / the kiln is cold and
distant / your fingers are caressing knives / words
warp the clay / the tether is suffocating and
unbearable / there is nothing perfect by your
hands / you divine this was all for the best /
regrets aside / bitterness can taste sweet if we
wish it so / and we drink deeply from the muddied
waters / we drink until our bellies are swollen / a
sickness / full of bees and stones and sticks / we
drink until we have no choice / we see you for
what you are / we are unmade from your image /
the sum of our relationship is death and rebirth /
the average of our love / loss.

THE FLOWER POT
IS EMPTY

we will never be enough / for you / love is an empty flower pot / always needing digging up / tending / ripping / tearing / 'make it pretty' / but there is nothing pretty / about two wolves / painted in mud / rooted little weeds / eyes of chamomile and poppies / hands of ivy / legs of leeks / spider lily locks / 'what a mess you've made' / 'how ugly you are' / 'you're no children of mine' / we will never be enough / for us / love is an empty flower pot / waiting to be filled and fixed / always needing pinched and plucked / always needing torn out by the roots / shaken out / put right.

A SMALL,
QUIET TRUTH.

We feared the silence more than the violence.

That we'd be nothing without you.

THERE IS HOPE

In the lost garden

the remains of our dreams sing

softly in the rain

FOR US, SOMEWHERE

失われた庭で

私たちの夢の遺跡が歌う

雨の中でそっと

FAMILIARITY

There is a comfort in the darkness / the way like calls to like / silence knows us best / as if our hearts were rivers / bare and perceptible / meeting at a fated crossroads / as if these faces were carved from ivory and wood and glass / miniature grief, a circus of lips, eyes of smoke drowned by the rain / we stare, unsettled / Who is that? / Who is she? / Who are we? / "We're the same" / someone whispers / we hate it / we hate it so much / we pull the darkness tight against us, as if to banish a chill in the air / how does one escape the icy course of DNA? / the undeniable company of history frozen in our bones? We give it a name, a talisman, a disguise to trick ourselves / we call it "comfort" / we call it "home" / we say it's all we'll ever know.

THE LANGUAGE OF FORGETTING

And suddenly, our existence was quietly bearable / time is swallowed by the bloodied muscle / unnecessaries burrowed in the esophagus / violence simmering to stillness sleeps / waiting / wanting / watching / the mirror pivots inward / we retreat into the alien tundra of self / the past is not faded / distant whisper / like a scar smoothed to silver lines on a map / our tongue chewed into submission / unwilling to disturb the room / lest the dust unsettle / gods help us /reminding us why this reprieve is survival / forgiveness is sucking the emotion from the marrow / blind ourselves just to see / we crawl inside this false shell / lovely hollow of intricate meaning/ bliss-blessed / quaint ignorance /fragile glass dream.

what is love,

what is motherhood,

what is unforgivable

LETTER 0

Our tongues were
useless / mumbled
hymns / bled on
prayer / lied until
flesh was blue /
cowered / slithered
pride / cut /
s w a l l o w e d
unkindness /
writhed in ivory
tombs / coiled /
those mournful
creatures / buried
deep in split lips /
sunken welts /
useless little knives.

Poet's notes: *Conversations With NASA* is a braided nonfiction essay structured as a transcripted dialogue between celestial objects in the Milky Way Galaxy and NASA. Using fragmentation, lush style, and symbolism, each planet contains a memory from the past, present, or future where the narrator struggles to find logic in a seemingly senseless universe. The objects in space become symbols of crucial moments that are paralleled by NASA's attempt to use whatever it already knows about astronomy to understand them. However, as the tug o' war between dialogue becomes complex, the conversations are left vulnerable for readers to decide whether or not there are logical answers.

Conversations With NASA challenges the authority of family, addressing issues of abuse, drug use, and mental health in the 90s, while attempting to understand them through the rational lens of science. My intention with this piece was to expose the contradictory nature of the human heart, which seems to defy logic in a physical world bound by it. As readers might note, the planets are not in the expected order, a structure that defies some of the logic NASA imparts. Jupiter is missing entirely, representing something so vast and uncontainable that there are no words. Like grief, its absence is a hole in the universe that can't be overlooked or ignored, but it also can't be explained.

CONVERSATIONS
with NASA

[EARTH]: You say this is how a mother loves her children: Embrace. Bruise. Blind. Apologies. Wounds. Distance. Forgiveness. Regression. The umbilical cord is gravity; the dance between child and mother repeats, the difference between life and death begins in the womb. It is there, you said, you came to love me; you dreamed of me, regretted me, thought of ending me. You say a mother will tear her body apart for her children. You say a mother will forgive her children anything. You say a mother only knows how to love her children without condition; You say I am you and you are me and we will always be tethered by this gravity. You say this is how we began and how we will end.

> **[NASA]:** The Roche Limit is the closest a celestial body can get without being torn apart by the tidal gravity of a planet. It is dangerous for debris in space to pass too close to the Earth. Moons, asteroids, meteors, and even man-made satellites in space can be drawn in by gravity and torn apart. This is how a planet gets its ring. This is how shooting stars fall to Earth. This is how the molecules for life began. This is how the dinosaurs died. This is a possibility for future extinction.

[ASTEROID BELT]: "X" marks the spot where I buried our photos for safekeeping. I dig them up once a year to find the five of us posing, a mother and her four daughters. One is screaming her head off impatiently. One is distracted by a lazy bee buzzing closer. One is leaning forward, eager for attention. One is tucked in the back like a bookmark, playing with her hair. Despite the squabbles, the mother will sing to her children as she cleans the house; she will dance and laugh when her husband isn't home; she will take them all to the beach that day, soaking in the golden rays and warm sands. Her children will complain of the heat, but they savor the moment; they choose to stay like this: happy.

> **[NASA]:** The Asteroid Belt contains billions of asteroids made of rock, ranging from the size of pebbles to massive, boulderous chunks. Located between Mars and Jupiter, these rocks are easily swayed by gravitational pulls. Sometimes we call them planets; sometimes they're nothing except dust, but we view them with wonder all the same.

[INTL SPACE STATION]: Tell me the story again; the one where we escape the fate of the place we've tried so hard to leave behind. Say we arrived on cloud nine, where every scar made, every unkindness uttered, is forgotten. Tell me the war of blood and ghosts is over, and this steel cage we've built will be enough. We will be enough. Won't we? Won't we? Tell me there is nothing in the known universe that could destroy this place we've come to call home. Promise me this will be our first horizon, our final frontier. Swear this is the part where we never abandon the mission. Let me rest my head in your lap while we dare to dream, and you tell me the story again: the one where we're free from the weight that's torn us apart. We are starlight, briefly beautiful, even in all the darkness. Say this is how we begin, again and again.

> **[NASA]:** The third brightest object in the night sky, the International Space Station was launched in 1998 and has been inhabited continuously for over 19 years. It is the 9th of such stations that conducts research into not only astrophysics and space equipment, but also human physiology and the impact of living in zero gravity for extended periods of time. It is only through experiments conducted at the ISS that we understand the potential consequences of radiation, long-term isolation, weightlessness, and confinement.

[NEPTUNE]: You say i am the star of my father's eye, born in 1989, and that is why we never got along. We are cold as ice, prone to inconsistent stupors of introversion, and uncommonly restless. It's impossible to speak to us because we are alien, and our language is in symbols and divination. Quadruple blue eyes watching you with distant judgment. Erudites. Children of the Wind. Quick to leave before we've even arrived.

> **[NASA]:** Farthest from the sun, it takes Neptune 164 years to complete a single orbit and 18 hours to complete a rotation on its axis. Though it is the smallest of all the Ice Giants, Neptune is the coldest world in the entire solar system. The largest recorded storm, known as the

Great Dark Spot, was in 1989 and lasted about five years.

[OORT CLOUD]: She and I shared everything: a bed, a bath, a mother. We chased each other from room to room, surviving on dreams. We built a clubhouse together. We climbed trees together. We fought and loved together. At night, when we were too afraid to fall asleep, we held hands together. Everything came in twos - pajamas, Christmas presents, tantrums, heartache. A hunger for destruction and proficiency for bad memory.

> **[NASA]:** Our scientists believe the Oort Cloud to be as old as the formation of the Milky Way Galaxy, and the place of Origin for all comets in this system. This sphere of celestial dust and ice is theorized to be the birth place and the remains of what once formed the sun and its planets. The scattering of this cloud is thought to be the result of Jupiter's immense gravity as it formed. We refer to objects in the Oort Cloud as "Trans-Neptunian" objects.

[ERIS]: Our house was the yellow one with blue shutters. Pine trees gathered around and bent over the shingled roof. Grandmother tried to work the earth, but the soil was infertile; it was sulfuric clay the color of rusted sunsets. The water tasted of pennies. The dry walls were scribbled with notes. The floors held all the secrets, with its holes and creaks and scratches. Voices raised like nails on glass. Screen doors slammed like slaps to the face. Cigarettes glowed like branding prods. Vacant eyes loomed over breakfast plates. Papaw's belt is missing; there is red wax under my mother's fingernails; everyone pretends not to notice the puncture marks in the wooden table.

[NASA]: Named after the Goddess of Strife and Discord, Eris is the second largest of the dwarf planets. Originally, scientists thought the planet was bigger due to its incredibly bright red aura. Occasionally, Eris passes closer to the Sun than Pluto when its orbit is in Perihelion, but during its Aphelion, it's so distant, it passes beyond the Kuiper Belt system. It is said Eris was once locked into the belt, but was pried out by Neptune's gravitational pull. Eris has only one moon, Dysnomia, whose name was inspired by the Greek God's daughter of "lawlessness." In English, it also refers to a condition affecting the memory of words and naming things.

[PLUTO]: In 2006, you were finally released from prison. The news was scribbled on the back of a 17th birthday card in large, loopy cursive. "I'm coming to get you, baby." I moved into a new foster home in the middle of nowhere, to a crumbling town called Rimersburg. Population 894. It was filled with empty churches on every street. It was cold, even in the summer. It was dirty, no matter how much they tried to keep it clean. Misery loves company, they said. The devil does, too. You kept writing. I put your letters in a desk drawer. I kept taking my medicine. You kept "coming" well into 2007. I aged out of the system. You got married. It was the loneliest year.

[NASA]: Originally the ninth planet in the solar system, Pluto was reclassified as a dwarf planet in 2006 when it failed to meet the requirements. Covered in ice and dirt, it is considered the loneliest celestial body in the galaxy because of its unusually long orbit around the Sun and distance from the planets. It takes about three hours for sunlight to reach the distant dwarf planet.

[MERCURY]: It takes a whole house to raise children; when the mothers disappear in the middle of the night for a line of coke and faceless fathers are spoken of only in cuss-words spelled out, a grandmother is left behind to raise the children right. When you left again, for love or lust or a hit of something in between, I'd forgotten you by accident. Wrinkled, worn hands brought the world to me; they fed me, bathed me, and worked without pause. Those hands taught me to touch everything as if my own hands would be my survival. This is how you build, they showed me. This is how you give and take. With spitfire spirit, grandma had to overcome the curveballs you'd thrown at her and then the obstacles her grandchildren brought, but she was steel teeth and callused handed, mind sharper than any knife and heart deeper than any ocean. She embraced the second motherhood with stoicism. This is how we live, she said. A daughter is a daughter is a daughter, and we do what we must to raise them. Even when they abandon you.

> **[NASA]:** Mercury is the smallest planet and the closest to the sun. It is heavily composed of metals and rock, making it the second densest planet. Unlike all the other planets, which are able to "self-heal" through geological processes, Mercury is the most battered with craters and wrinkles. It is named after the Roman messenger to the gods, who was the god of travelers, divination, and thieves.

[VENUS]: A second daughter is born in 1991. You call her love at first sight, the greatest fruition of your efforts. You call her your second chance, your last hope, beautiful redemption. You say her first cry was the moment you knew life was beautiful, her first words were a sign that good things were possible for people like us. She was your beginning and your end, and no matter how many times she burned, cursed, ruined, or hurt you, the pain was worth it. This is love, you said. This is motherhood. You believed with all your heart she was the beautiful dream to end life's nightmare.

> **[NASA]:** Venus is the second brightest object in the sky, often referred to as Morning Star or Evening Star, because it was originally thought to have been two separate celestial bodies in the sky. Because of its dense atmosphere of sulfuric acid, the surface of Venus was hidden from sight, fueling the belief that the planet was a tropical paradise. Our scientists once dreamed of traveling to its mysterious surface, but during the 1960s, we discovered its hostile environment; it is uninhabitable.

[MARS]: The first pill I ever swallowed was white as snow. The second was red. The third was the color of my flesh. The fourth was blue as a bruise. The fifth as pink as the rim around my eyes. There were others with colors I didn't have names for. All met at the base of my stomach with the rush of water. To be better. To be sterile. To be enough. To be whole. To be me, whoever that was. I couldn't swallow them all at once; I had to choke them down. I thought of you every time one got stuck at the back of my throat. I think I did it because I loved you.

[NASA]: Mars is called the "Red Planet" due to its blood-red color. Because of its unusually elongated elliptical orbit around the sun, Mars produces the largest dust storms that last for months and more extreme seasons than most of the other planets. Scientists have found pieces of Mars embedded in the earth after being ejected from the planet millions of years ago. For years, scientists have speculated whether it is possible to inhabit the planet, with some arguing it is impossible while others claim it is. In the future, there will be a single ring around the planet when its moon, Phobos, breaches the Roche Limit and is torn apart by Mars' gravity.

[HALLEY'S COMET]: When I think about it, I wonder if I should be glad or afraid that we are built from hardier materials. Seven heart attacks. Four strokes. Six cases of cancer. Five documented cases of mental illness. Three generations of dementia. Two stubborn diabetics. Blood Pressure the size of skyscrapers. Blinder than bats. Innumerable car accidents. Two fires. Two wars. Lines of coke. Shots of booze. The endless game of psych med roulette. It's a miracle we're still alive. It's a miracle we haven't killed each other yet. I ponder endless ways to escape these fates.

[NASA]: Halley's Comet has been recorded since the times of ancient Greece. Visible to the naked eye from Earth, it is the only comet a human is likely to witness twice in a single lifetime. The ancients thought it to be an omen of great and terrible calamity. It's description: visible just after sunset in the western sky, fiery, head facing north, fast, icy, gaseous. It inspired the Italian painter Giotto's Star of Bethlehem in "The Adoration of the Magi while simultaneously sending whole civilizations into a panic.

[SATURN]: Memories are fickle, fragmented, and fragile. Our film is doubly exposed, predisposed to sudden blank reels and poor chemical reactions during development, but this is all we have; we find ways to make the pieces fit. A mother who looks like Julia Roberts. Pine sap on worn hands that work through hair on tiny heads. A paper cup of rainbow pills that taste bitter. An ocean rushing over four small feet rooted side-by-side. Bruises. The words "I hate you", "I miss you", "Am I enough?", and "I never want to see you again" overlay until they sound the same, wounding and promising hope all at once. A sickness and a cure. An intimate stranger. The dance between child and mother repeats.

[NASA]: Saturn is the most distant object in the sky that can be seen with the naked eye. It is most famous for its colorful atmospheric bands and its extensive ring system, which are made up of ice and organic matter known as carbonaceous dust. These rings, as mentioned before, were likely formed when celestial bodies traveled too close to the planet's Roche Limit and were torn apart by Saturn's gravitational pull.

[URANUS]: There is much to say and little time, so I listen. I unfold the crinkled letters and read them. They still smell of you, and I imagine I can touch you as I trace your words. You tell me about the past, of your first love who overdosed, of the girl you used to be and the fear you had growing up in that house. You tell me about the baby you never gave birth to, about all the mistakes you made with my father, the anger you've held between your lungs. You cry as you unfold the willful blindness, alcoholism, and abuse. You write "I love you" again and again, as if you know I'm leaving soon. You're sorry for abandoning me. You miss me. How am I doing? You're so proud of me. Am I there? Here? Anywhere? You tell me about the daughter of a daughter of a daughter who made all the wrong choices. Your regret is a garden, you said. It is a mansion, a library, a grave. But I am not one of them; you're so glad I'm not one of them.

> **[NASA]:** Uranus is perhaps one of the most peculiar of all the planets. Not only does the planet rotate in a retrograde direction, but it also spins on its side. In 1986, after a decade of space travel, the Voyager 2 relayed the first images of Uranus, but these images led only to more questions about its dim blue color and razor thin rings. When it was first discovered, Uranus was almost given the name Neptune.

We will be the blade

and the hand and the heart

of darkness, we will not

quietly fade into

the fiery pits of this world,

its selfish existence.

sometimes

all we can do is take a breath,

and brace for the wave.

AN INHERITANCE OF
LOVE MAPS

sharpness

       of closure on a lonely road at 3AM

streetlights bathe us in light but shadows cling

       inevitable lovers

tell us

       of the uncharted youth

    trailer park off the turnpike

     taste of moonshine

      Walmart dresses

aquarium of cuss words

    unfaithful fathers roaming

      stray cats and semitrucks

    coke dancing on glass

white and red stripes of the flag

        duty, honor, family

  $200 an hour

      cry so hard it sounds like laughter

   re-runs of *We're All Happy Here*

      late-night bonfire gatherings

do as we say, not as we do

     even if we are full of unwanted babies

eat the food on the table

             belt

 absence

    recollections too soft to keep

We cannot use our sharpened tongues without cutting our own cheeks. Our mouths are temples of scar tissue, taste of blood—relief, regret.

Part IV.
ROOTS

WE NEVER SETTLE

Rip them out by the roots, she says.
Don't count them petals—love me, not.
When the body grieves in the heat,
fingernails ache, crack, bleed,
inhale the earth as though being
buried is the only way to breathe.
Don't sacrifice your garden
For a handful of pretty weeds.

PARADISE FOUND

If my heart was a seashell, you
would be the ocean that carries me.
You would be the
sunlight, the endless blue sky,
horizon adventure. You
would be the message in a bottle that
arrives after a
shipwreck, a reminder that I am
never alone. If my heart was a
seashell, you could hold it to
your ear and hear
all the happiness you've given to me.

SERPENTINE

We crawled into each other's scars and wept
our pain was inseparable, our dreams a flame
our bodies frail yet unyielding, we entangled
little serpents in the dirt of memories
until the skin we wore sloughed away,
until nakedness wasn't death, but life
Until all that remained was the rawness
of being seen and not discarded
by the hands we dared to grasp.

the hardest part was realizing

it was okay to love you and still leave you.

~ breaking the cycle

THE YELLOW HOUSE

There is a place in our heart that will never heal.

That's okay, it's the only proof that we're even real.

That the home you worked so hard to build

    with cracked windows

        cold wooden floors

          kerosene heaters in
          corridors

              rusty knobs &
              wailing pipes

    curtains that let in the night

IN THE WOODS

A leaky basement filled with dust

Half-finished walls that were "just" enough

     doors hanging on hinges,
desperately,

This was the home you gave to us

and it was better than

     nothing, nothing, nothing.

OF ROOTS & FISSURES

The first memory we have of you is absence;

you were a crater, an empty well in the center

of us.

We waited in vain, fed on your promises,

Clung like regretful ghosts on your sleeves.

A WISH

I clasp my hands, and wait, wish, will for the days, when courage rises from the cold earth in my lung-cage, and I learn to let go of the loss I inherited from this broken garden of fear, and these hands grieve, grasp, grow to reach all the places I long to be.

WE, WINTER

tonight when it snows

this needless mountain we

carry in our soul will

shudder and collapse

teeth, exposed to wind

eyes, glassy exposition

bodies, submerged, clinging

a prayer for beginnings

an exhale of grief.

And it was then

that we finally understood

there could be no light

without the darkness.

LOVE

IS

A

LONG

GOODBYE

We will shed this grief / soured milk spilled over raw honey / the way flowers abandon their petals / trees exile their leaves / wind thins, chills, howls / bones a song of shivers and chatters / hands fisted in firs / lodged in teeth / we will shake the memories that haunt us / empty chairs / hollow rooms / whiskey bottles sparkling in sunlight / sunken tongues unable to say / goodbye, goodbye / our lost / we will shed this grief / in hymns, mutters, silent stares / we will carry you in nothing / our hearts / we will bury you in nothing / our love.

MOTHER, MOTHER

We longed to flourish in your shadow
content in being unseen, unknown,
instead of the bright gaze that always
found inadequate cracks in our clay

those gentle hands that shaped us
curled in contempt, ashamed
to have given us life.

could have been
would have been
should have been

FERAL GRIEF

We bared our teeth / milk blood and bourbon / soaked curses slid / bone raw / knife to lungs / claws rooted to the earth / frigid / rain-blind pitch / it wasn't rage / we snarl / it wasn't hate / we coil / it wasn't fear / we lunge / grief.

LET US DEPART

Our scars will tell the story the way a map draws a line from here to the end of the world: a fragmented tapestry that can only be appreciated from afar and interpreted by those who understand the language of wolves and the wild. We will not promise this is the beginning because it is also an end, but we will endure it. We will set sail for better things. We will make a life together no matter where we go. Home is a body is a vessel is a moment in time. It is you and I and we, together. And we are always there, half in shadow and half in light. Not good, but whole. Splintered, but repaired. It is enough. It is enough.

DEATH SONG

In the vibrant spring

like raindrop-soaked bitter earth

our bright bones did sing

死の歌

活気のある春に
雨滴に浸した苦い地球のように
私たちの明るい骨は歌いました

A SLOW, SURE END
IN THE FUTURE

Suffice to say, that feeling is in the air now. As if grief has arrived before the wound. Like death is coming slowly & all you can do is wait.

PROMISES, PROMISES

You promised us a future outside these faux wood panels / fir tree shadows cocooning our childhood / prison bars / skipping record regrets / gasoline dreams buried under cracked concrete / home built on sulfur and cigarettes / babies crying at 2am for mothers lost to the coke-blessed nights / there there, little ones / all will be well by morning / this is only a phase / a temporary nightmare / a passing fall from grace / we will escape this place together / we will never be like them / we will triumph over this legacy / we will have everything we longed for / it kills us to stay / these rooms are claustrophobic / the clock is broken / we linger / we wait / you promised us.

WE ARE NOT HOME

We are not where you left us / caught between turbulent seasons / child, woman, mother / we are beyond the fence of our youth / treading the wild world / predatory caught / shivering eagerness / hungry to own / to name / to be / do not knock on the door / no one is home to greet you / no one is there / waiting under the soft embrace of shadows / for the kiss of validation on our brows / the lead hand of acknowledgment / gaze of pride and kindest words / we are freed as swallows in the field / we are light as the breeze cutting grass / unsettling wishing flowers / soaking in sunlight and dew / we are not where you left us / protected and alone and miserable / cocooned by jealousy and greed / there is no golden cage to hold us / we are not afraid / we are not where you left us.

LETTER X

Like a woody cone,

    Evolved

with scales and spikes,

    We, too, have grown

armor,

    To protect

What remains.

FUNERAL DAUGHTERS

There is a song in our hearts, and it is your name.

In between sips of sweet wine, we mourn it.

We repeat the epic of your life out loud,

an opera of sorrow, an ode to myth, a cycle of

redemption, because the hum of grief

is still too distant to hear

There is only the ocean chewing the coast.

There is only the mountain looming unchanged.

There is only this ash and whiskey hymn.

There is only us left behind, carrying you home.

Let us stay in the presence of your memory,

if only for a moment longer.

AWAY, NEVER NEAR

We are not the children they abandoned to the wilds of this world / we are light as air / silky as water / bright as the tendrils of sunlight threading through the trees / there is a place we go to laugh / there is a place we go to cry / there is a place we go to hide from the burdens of being born / but it is a place we go / together, together, together / come, come / she says / pulling my hand / closeness warm as a wool cape / fingers strong as knotted sinew / eyes like hazel lighthouses guiding us back to life / this is where we belong / this is where we learned to love / this is who we need to be / this is how we forgive / we will never be them / no matter what.

COLLECTIVE JOY AND SORROW

departure

           we will never be enough

      to temper the sting

            your discontent

    is a slow-killing poison

           we loved to drink

love us?

       or not?

relief

              Joy

    freedom

        are the realization

     that we have become   *more than clay*

that our legacies live

        beyond your shadow of doubt

we will never be good little girls

         holy little wolves

content daughters of the kiln

     or you,   *but we will*   *be*   *whole*

...shall we endure together?

ARI AUGUSTINE

 Ari Augustine is an editor, poet, and writer of spec fic, where she lurks in the darker forests of adult SFF. She is the creator of Bookish Valhalla and a speaker on the Empathy For The Devil WriteHive 2021 panel. She adores getting lost between the dusty shelves of used bookshops, but her favorite places to disappear to are museums, historical landmarks, and video games. Ari holds a B.A. in English Lit from the Univ. of WA. She lives in the wilds of Tennessee with her husband and their two feline guardians of the void, Little Fury and Mori-kun. *HALF LIGHT* is her sophomore poetry collection, set to release Winter 2022. Though Ari often vanishes from the human realm without warning, you can summon her on Twitter or her website.

www.ariaugustine.com/books
www.twitter.com/soufflelumiere
www.instagram.com/soufflelumiere/

OTHER BOOKS BY ARI AUGUSTINE

Elsewhere, We Became

An original collection of poetry that explores the intricacies of identity, loss, and how humans define "home". Augustine's darkly lyrical poetry and prose are refreshingly bold, weaving together childhood loss, evolving identities, and the shifting views of love. Elsewhere, We Became exposes the strange messiness of life through a kaleidoscope lens of a girl on the hunt for her place in the world.

https://www.amazon.com/Elsewhere-We-Became-Ari-Augustine-ebook/dp/B07CR7V9BN/

ACKNOWLEDGMENTS

Many thanks to the divine universe for never failing to feed my creative soul and haunting me with muses. To the writing community online for its quiet appreciation of cryptic 3AM poetic lines that anyone else would call 911 over. To the polar bears of my childhood who protected, advocated, and always listened. To the Diabolical Writers Guild, Avhlee Guyton-White, Alexandria Diamond, and Amanda Brown for the warm memories we've made through the winters of life. Apologies and thanks to my husband for having to put up with me drinking whiskey and reciting poetry out loud for hours on end. It really must be love. To K.J. Harrowick for not only the design of this collection, but also her close friendship, dark humor, and kickass creative mind. I also want to thank my grandmother, who planted the seeds of resilience, exploration, and finding the wonder in ordinary things. And lastly, to you, for enduring all this time.

HALF
LIGHT

ANEMOIA